DATING HACKS HANDBOOK

HOW TO DEAL WITH THE WORST CASE SITUATIONS OF MODERN LOVE

DRAGON FRUIT

MARIA LLORENS AND HUGO VILLABONA

Maria Llorens and Hugo Villabona/Mango Media, Inc.
2525 Ponce de Leon, Suite 300
Coral Gables, FL 33134
www.mangomedia.us

Publisher's Note: This is a work of humor with a hint of self-help.
The authors wish to thank all the experts, guides and experiences which
were considered during the writing process.

Dating Hacks Handbook / Maria Llorens and Hugo Villabona. -- 1st ed.
ISBN 978-1-63353-063-8

DISCLAIMER

Dating can be complicated, but we've broken down the best and worst of it to make it as easy as can be. From your first online dating profile to making a long-term relationship work, we've got the information you need to make love last. Our hacks don't shy away from the both the fun parts of romance and its dark sides.

If you're a girl, guy, neither, both, gay, straight, bi, or everything in between—this guide is for you. We've tried to get every perspective under the sun on romantic endeavors. Everyone needs to be loved (or just lusted after), and there's no one right way to do it. The advice in this book covers the common threads within all relationships, no matter what your path is to romantic bliss. We can't find you "the one," but we can give you the tools to try. Whether your goal is finding true love or enjoying eternal "singledom", we've got a hack for it.

"But now I know the things I know
And do the things I do,
And if you do not like me so,
To hell, my love, with you."

— Dorothy Parker

CONTENTS

PREFACE

The world is full of bad dating advice and conventional wisdom. Well, no more! Dating Hacks Handbook is the 21st century gender-neutral dating bible you've always wanted. Forget boring advice like what you should wear and when to pop the question, we're giving you the most practical solutions to all the weird and typical questions you've ever had about dating. Stuff like: Where should we go on a date? How often should I mention my cats on my OkCupid profile? When do I bring up my handcuff fetish?

To all these questions and more, we've come up with easy, not-awkward ways to make dating smooth sailing for everyone involved. And for the possibly dangerous, intimate side of dating—we've got plenty of advice for when you hit a tough spot.

We can't promise you'll find that eternal soul mate, but we can assure a few romantic evenings and plenty of stories to tell to the homeless man on the subway.

CHAPTER 1 //
Looking for Lovin'

**Looking for Lovin' //
Should I Date?**

It's easy to look out into the world and envy swarms of couples, both real and fictional, who parade around smiling and laughing and feeling superior to singletons. But are you actually ready for that kind of responsibility?

Like a tower of shaky Jenga pieces, your potential relationship will only be as strong as you and whomever you choose to share your life.

Ready for a Relationship?

Do you have time?

There are only 24 hours in a day. Maybe you work, or study, or both. Then you have to give your dog a bath, give yourself a bath (maybe simultaneously to save time), and make dinner. Oh, hi laundry. Your best friend is in a slump and wants to talk for 3 hours. The new season of The Walking Dead is piling up on your DVR. Can you fit another human being into that schedule? No one knows, really.

Do you care?

Human beings have needs. They like to be hugged, eat pizza, and leave the house once in a while. Sometimes they need other people to do those things. Do you have the energy to wonder if your potential partner is happy? Are you even going to remember to ask?

Can you compromise?

In a relationship, you're trying to combine your life and values with your partner's. This can feel like slamming two round pegs into one square hole at the same time, and sometimes the pegs are made of tears, and it's really hard to work with those.

Can you communicate?

This goes hand-in-hand with caring. Are you able to articulate why you're happy or not happy? Are you able to listen patiently when your partner does the same? Can you do both of those things without yelling? Do you have a desire to hit people when they disagree with you? Are human beings irritating and confusing to you?

Where are you going?

You can't always predict where life is taking you, but if you think you're going to make a big change in your life soon—less than a few months—then reconsider jumping into something serious.

Who to Date?

If you've decided that you can possibly include someone new in your life, then what kind of person do you want to date?

It's not a great idea to keep a set list of arbitrary deal breakers in your head. These can range from standards for physical appearance to education to economic status. All of these can be pretty snobby and limiting parameters to set for yourself – and could keep you away from someone worthwhile.

But it is a good idea to reflect on what kind of relationship would make you happy. Short-term? Long-term? Monogamous? Do you want to have long conversations about books? Do you want someone who enjoys the outdoors? Are you religious?

Think about your values, hobbies, and emotional needs. Knowing yourself first can help you decide if someone is right for you.

Looking for Lovin' //
Plenty of Fish

Now that you've reflected on your needs and desires, it's time to find a date! But where do you look for the elusive, interesting single someone?

There are so many options, it's hard to know where to start, but once you do you can get your game plan rolling. The key to finding a good match is exploring different places, activities, and even apps that are specific to what you want.

Where to Find a Date

Your friends.

No, don't date your friends (unless you really want to open that can of worms), but use their social network to expand your own. Go out and grab a drink or join them in a group activity or hobby. Meeting new people is easier with someone to vouch for your sanity and likability.

Bars.

It's the usual approach, but you don't only have to go dancing and clubbing. Try your local bar on a trivia night or arcade night if that's more your speed. Go out, get some liquid courage (not too much), and talk to a cutie about video games.

Dog parks.

Love animals? Turn your usual pet-related chores into an opportunity for love and strike up a conversation with a dog lover in between poop duties.

Go outside!

For you sports and outdoorsy types, find a group, class, or local team to make your exercise more social.

Classes.

Get out of the house and pursue your hobbies by taking a class. You can meet someone who shares your interests and learn something new.

Shopping.

Maybe not when you're stocking up on toilet paper, but if you're at a bookstore or a record store, strike up a conversation about a band or writer you love. Some stores, like comic book shops, host events or game nights.

Volunteering.

Doing some non-profit work can put you in touch with people who care about the same things you do, and you'll be helping others.

Conventions.

If you're into comic books, sci-fi, gaming, or some other nerdy niche hobby, look for a convention happening near you. Depending on the size, there can be thousands of like-minded singles in the same room. And some schedule speed-dating events as well.

Clubs.

Find a group for something you like, whether it's a book club or cycling club, and share your interests.

Meetups.

Sites like Meetup.com help you find gatherings of people who share a hobby or lifestyle. You'll also find singles meetups scheduled on the site.

Politics and activism.

If you've got an issue you're passionate about, share that with others. And if it's election season, help out with a campaign to meet people who also care about your community.

WARNING!

A few situations are best left untapped for possible dates. Or, at least, proceed with caution.

The office.

It's easy to fall for someone if you see them every day, but if it doesn't work out . . . you still see them every day. It could also be against your employer's rules or there could be ethical implications, depending on your line of work. If you're going to do it, the best time to date someone in your office is if one of you will be leaving the job soon.

School.

Not recommended. Teacher-student relationships happen, but they're pretty unprofessional and unethical. If you find yourself tempted, wait until the semester is over. You don't want your hard work tainted by anything inappropriate.

Power imbalance.

If you're someone's boss or their partner in a business or creative venture, dating is going to be fraught with complications. It's hard to separate work from love, and it's even harder if one of you has authority over the other.

If it wasn't clear enough already, the main concept here is to get out of the house. Take risks, meet new people, and try new things. Take a different bus route. Go somewhere in your city you've never seen. You'll feel refreshed and possibly meet someone worth asking out. Or you'll have a story to tell when you do find a date. If you're at home on Netflix, your only potential date is whoever is delivering your pizza (it's an option).

**Looking for Lovin' //
Your Online Persona**

S o, maybe you're shy about meeting people in real life or you want to expand your dating pool further—that's where online dating can help.

Online dating can be weird, disillusioning, and sometimes outright dangerous. You can't really help that the Internet is full of anonymous creeps. But it can also be exciting and fun if you approach it correctly. First things first, you need a profile.

All About You

Profile pic.

Smile in your profile picture (if you want to), it'll make you seem approachable. And look into the camera, people feel more connected that way.

Evidence.

You can say you're funny and interesting in your profile, but why should anyone believe you? Mention some personal anecdotes or facts that show what you're claiming.

Buzzwords.

Don't be something you're not, but keep in mind how you describe things and what you mention in your profile. Research shows words like "athlete," "sushi," and "driven" get a high attractiveness rating. (We don't get the sushi part either.)

Accomplishments.

You don't have to list your resume, but be confident about things you've done. People who mention college degrees get more hits.

Interests.

Show you're passionate about something, then go broad and list other hobbies and activities you like. Be specific. Everyone "likes movies." Do you like certain directors or genres? Mention those, too.

Ideal mate.

Talk about what kind of person you're looking for, but be general. Think about what you reflected on earlier. Long book conversations? Throw that in. Be honest about what kind of date would be fun for you.

Liar, liar.

Don't lie about details like your height and weight. Or anything, really. You want to attract someone who likes you the way you are. Kick anyone else to the digital curb.

TMI.

Generally, keep your profile positive. Think of it as your first introduction at a party—you're not dumping your soul out just yet. It doesn't have to be all rainbows, either. If you have a dark sense of humor or some other quirk, try to get that across in your profile.

Extra hack:

Write your profile in a Word or another program where you can use spell check. Check your grammar. Being literate is cool.

Remember, you don't have to include every detail about your life. And really, you shouldn't. Keep personal information out for safety reasons. There's plenty of time to get to know your dates. Balance making your profile the best version of you, but also an honest version. They'll get to know the real you in due time.

HIGHEST RANKED ACTIVITIES

The sexiest sports for your online profile.

MALES
RANK (OUT OF 1,000)

FEMALES
RANK (OUT OF 1,000)

01
Surfing

03
Yoga

03
Yoga

04
Surfing

04
Skiing

23
Running

57
Golf

50
Tennis

64
Biking

70
Dancing

66
Hiking

85
Biking

86
Running

GENDER IS OUTDATED

Users who list interests that aren't
typically masculine or feminine rank higher.

RANKINGS

"MY CHILDREN"
Males 44
Females 978

"ELECTRONICS"
Males 790
Females 49

"CRAFT"
Males 183
Females 912

THE INTERNET Does Not Apply

Once you get personal about your cats
everyone is weirded out. They're lame.

"CATS"
274

"MY CATS"
766

CALL ME A WOMAN, THANKS

Guys definitely shouldn't refer to women as girls. Neither
should women, though you get an edge if you do (thumbs
down, Internet). And learn your who's from your whom's.

It's **28%**
Better for a Male to refer to
Females as Women than Girls

It's **16%**
Better for a Female to refer to
herself as a Girl than a Woman

Men who use
"WHOM" get
31% more contact
from the opposite sex

WHEN TO LOG ON

Sundays are the best day to get some profile activity going.
Peak hours depend on what app you're using.

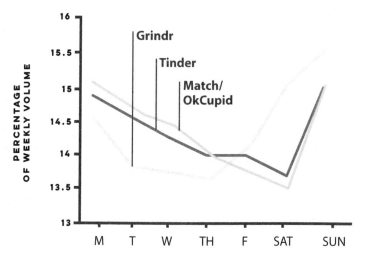

PEAK HOURS VARY

Grindr	Tinder	Match/OkCupid
		12 PM
		1 PM
░		2 PM
░		3 PM
		4 PM
		░ 5 PM
	▓	░ 6 PM
	▓	7 PM
	▓	░ 8 PM
		░ 9 PM
		10 PM

**Looking for Lovin' //
Grindr Your Grouper**

D ifferent dating services offer different experiences, so here's a quick rundown of how the best ones work:

Match.com

With 1.8 million users, Match.com offers a more serious dating pool since it's primarily a paid service (the free version doesn't offer as many tools). It works fairly traditionally – make a profile, check your matches, chat, and arrange a date.

OkCupid

As a free service, it's pretty much open season on the kinds of people you can find on OkCupid. That can mean a few weirdoes and jerks who send unwelcome messages. But the site boasts a good matching algorithm, stemming from the long list of questions you answer to start your profile. It also has mobile versions to take your matches on the go.

Tinder

Tinder is app-only and less comprehensive than the first two options. You won't be writing lengthy biographical details here or your favorite song lyrics. To sign up, you have to use your Facebook account—the app uses your activity to judge your potential matches. It's bare bones speed-dating. Swipe through matches until you find someone, and if you both match, chat away. Its lack of detail makes it known primarily for hookups, but you never know.

Grindr

Grindr is similar to Tinder, but caters only to men who are seeking men. Its main feature is utilizing GPS to find available guys near you. Unlike Tinder, you don't have to register with Facebook. Upload a nice picture and a short bio, and you're good to go. Like Tinder, it's primarily known for its hookup potential.

Grouper

Grouper sets up group dates for you and your friends. A group of three of you can sign up, for example, and one of you manages the account by answering a questionnaire. Grouper then chooses your dates, a location, and sends email and text updates. One caveat is cost. Each person pays about $17 for the service, so that's $51 for the three of you. But if you hate the usual one-on-one date setup, it might be a worthwhile service.

Coffee Meets Bagel

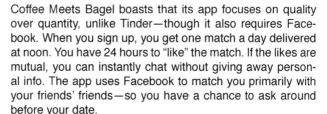

Coffee Meets Bagel boasts that its app focuses on quality over quantity, unlike Tinder—though it also requires Facebook. When you sign up, you get one match a day delivered at noon. You have 24 hours to "like" the match. If the likes are mutual, you can instantly chat without giving away personal info. The app uses Facebook to match you primarily with your friends' friends—so you have a chance to ask around before your date.

Online dating takes a lot of trial and error, so don't be too discouraged if your first attempts aren't stellar. Try out one or two at a time so it doesn't become a time-sucking obsession. There're only so many out-of-nowhere "DTF?" messages you can take.

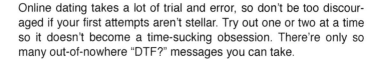

SURPRISING STATS ABOUT
ONLINE DATING

3 MOST COMMON METHODS OF INTRODUCTION

1 MUTUAL ACQUAINTANCE
2 WORK OR SCHOOL
3 MEET ONLINE

17% OF THOSE WHO MARRIED IN THE PAST THREE YEARS MET ONLINE

120,000
U.S. COUPLES
WHO MARRY EACH YEAR
MET ONLINE

INFIDELITY

90% OF PEOPLE IN **ONLINE AFFAIRS** GET ADDICTED TO THEM, BECOMING **SERIAL ONLINE CHEATERS**

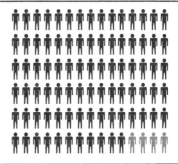

LIES IN THE PROFILE

WOMEN PUT A PREMIUM ON INCOME & HEIGHT WHEN DECIDING WHICH MAN TO CONTACT

80% LIED ABOUT THEIR **AGE, HEIGHT OR WEIGHT**

WEIGHT — 64% / 36%

HEIGHT — 42% / 56%

AGE — 13% / 87%

LYING ABOUT **SMOKING : HIGHLY UNACCEPTABLE!**

**Looking for Lovin' //
First Dates**

Y ou met a cutie and now you're ready to go on that first real-life
outing. First impressions are really nerve-wracking. What do you
wear? Where do you go? What should you talk about? Do you kiss?
It's enough to make you want to cancel and wait for a future where
mates are assigned to each other by a supreme overlord. But never
fear, we've got you covered:

Ace the Date

Location.

Grab a drink, coffee, or a low-key dinner. If you'd like
something more elaborate, check out the list below.

What to wear.

Dress like yourself and for the activity you chose.
And take a shower.

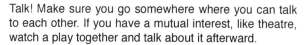

What to do.

Talk! Make sure you go somewhere where you can talk
to each other. If you have a mutual interest, like theatre,
watch a play together and talk about it afterward.

Time.

Don't plan a long, drawn-out affair. Be specific about what
you want to do and don't overextend your date.

What to say.

Get the usual questions – where you work, where you
went to school – out of the way quickly. Talk about things
you care about and mutual interests. Bring up a contro-
versial question or two to spice things up.

Listen.

Don't dominate the conversation. Ask genuine questions
and listen to your date.

Who pays?

Forget boring gender norms. If you initiated the date, you pay. If your date wants to split the bill, go ahead. Always plan ahead to pay for two.

If they paid?

Don't feel obliged to do anything you don't want to just because someone bought you dinner. If you want to even things out a bit, offer to buy drinks.

Awkward is okay.

All first dates are a little awkward—embrace it. Laugh off the tension by admitting you're a little nervous.

Keep your head.

It's your choice, but maybe avoid getting very drunk on the first date. You're trying to pay attention to this person and decide if you like them.

Kiss?

If things are going well and your date seems open to it— go for it. Wait until you're closer to the end of the date. And if your date is a guy, don't necessarily wait for him to take the lead.

A little more?

Up to you and your date. There's no rule as to whether it'll work if you wait to have sex. You may celebrate your 80th anniversary decades after that night. Or not. Life's a gamble.

Part two?

If you had a good time (or if you didn't), say so. Be direct, but not pushy, about wanting to see your date again.

Beyond Basics

You can go beyond the simple coffee or drinks, but run your ideas by your date first. Showing you care about their interests will make a good impression before you even leave the house.

- Bowling
- Aquarium
- Amusement park
- Art museum
- Zoo
- Rock climbing
- Sports game
- Theatre
- Arcade
- Observatory stargazing
- Concert

MOST POPULAR ON-DEMAND DATING LOCATIONS

Top 30 Locations

1. Starbucks
2. Chipotle Mexican Grill
3. Panera Bread
4. The Cheesecake Factory
5. Texas Roadhouse
6. Buffalo Wild Wings
7. Olive Garden
8. Chili's Grill & Bar
9. In-N-Out Burger
10. Applebee's
11. Blue Bottle Coffee
12. LongHorn Steakhouse
13. Five Guys
14. BJ's Restaurant and Brewhouse
15. Peet's Coffee & Tea
16. Red Lobster
17. Tim Hortons
18. Outback Steakhouse
19. Philz Coffee
20. Tender Greens
21. Yard House
22. P.F. Chang's
23. Yogurtland
24. Dutch Bros. Coffee
25. Torchy's Tacos
26. Mellow Mushroom
27. Bareburger
28. Cracker Barrel Old Country Store
29. 16 Handles
30. California Pizza Kitchen

MOST POPULAR ON-DEMAND DATING LOCATIONS

Top Categories by Gender

Men prefer to meet at **RESTAURANTS** on a first date

Restaurants	CoffeeShops	Bars
51%	**31%**	**18%**

Women prefer to meet at **COFEESHOPS** on a first date

CoffeeShops	Restaurants	Bars
52%	**35%**	**13%**

FIRST DATE FOOD AND DRINK RULES CONTINUED

How many alcoholic beverages are acceptable for your date to have on the first date?

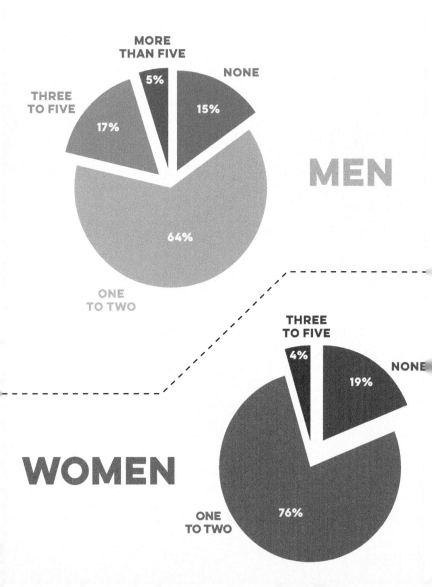

MEN

- MORE THAN FIVE 5%
- NONE 15%
- THREE TO FIVE 17%
- ONE TO TWO 64%

WOMEN

- THREE TO FIVE 4%
- NONE 19%
- ONE TO TWO 76%

**Looking for Lovin' //
Date Two?**

So your first date is over, and you're frantically checking your phone for new messages. Will they call back? Are you dreading it if they do? Here's how to handle the post-date aftermath:

"Hey :D"

To text or not to text.

Don't be shy about wanting to see your date again, but don't come on too strong, either. Something like, "I had a great time yesterday, hope we can go out again soon," should do the trick. Add emoticons at your leisure.

Que sera, sera.

If your date doesn't write back or gives you a lukewarm response—let it go. If you've been clear about your intentions, it's probably a no. There are plenty of other opportunities out there.

Nope, negative, nein.

If you had a terrible time or you just didn't click with your date, be honest with them if they contact you. Thank them for the date and wish them luck in the future, but admit you don't think it'll work out.

Friendzone'd

The "friend zone," as some like to call it, is not a real thing. Sorry, lovebirds, but friendship isn't a consolation prize for not getting nooky. If your first date is a dud, you can opt to be friends. Don't offer to be a friend if you don't want to be, especially if it's out of false hope. That's a waste of everyone's time. And be respectful of acquaintances or friends who turn down even the first date.

If you do want to be friends after the date, tell them you had a great time but you feel you'd prefer to be friends. Maybe you'll have a new BFF if they agree.

CHAPTER 2 //
DIGITAL ROMANCE

**Digital Romance //
Safe Sexting**

When mankind learned we could draw our junk on the wall of a cave, we did. Many, many times. Today, we put our phones' cameras to the same use. It's a sign of affection, titillation, and a bit of showing off what you got. Chances are you'll send a few sexy pics in the course of your dating life. Here are a few things to think about before you sext:

Risk and reward.

Once you send out a picture of yourself, you really don't have control over it anymore. Make sure you really trust the recipient of your noodz.

Forever. And ever.

And, well, if you don't trust them, be okay with the fact that those pictures could suddenly appear online and everyone you know could see them. Everyone.

Headless hottie.

It's recommended to leave out easily recognizable body parts or markings out of your photos. Like your face. It's okay, you're just as sexy without a head. Really.

Prurient politeness.

No one wants to see you naked. Unless they do. They actually said so. You can send your naked pictures to those people.

Sketchy apps.

Check the security of the apps you're using to send pictures. Even staples like Snapchat aren't immune to security failures. Definitely avoid 3rd party apps that claim to add extra features to Snapchat and other apps—in October 2014 they were the cause of a massive leak of users' photos.

Encrypt your $%*#:

Apps like Cover Me make your texts private, so your pictures can't be tied to you later (provided your face isn't in them). That said, it can't stop someone from taking a screenshot.

Before you post.

Don't be quick to post anything. If you're keeping your nudes in the same device as your regular photos, it could end up going in a text to Mom. Or worse, Twitter.

Be trustworthy.

Don't be that jerk who posts private pictures on revenge sites or shares them with other people. Someone is trusting you with their most intimate details, enjoy responsibly.

Brave new nudes.

Don't make fun of people whose pictures get leaked online— even celebrities. It could be you any day now. Be part of a nicer world where we don't shame people for having a normal sex life.

Protect your junk.

It's public knowledge (thanks, Edward Snowden!) that NSA surveillance can get access to most of your digital correspondence, including the sexy kind. Especially on that crazy trip to the Bahamas. National security questions aside, it's something to consider before you click "send."

With an estimated 54% of Americans ages 18-54 tapping away at their phones for some lewd lovin', you're not alone in this risky behavior. Just keep in mind that there are consequences, both private and public. It's up to you to decide if it matters.

LOVE IN THE AGE OF TECHNOLOGY

BREAKING UP WITH YOUR DATA

PRIVATE DATA, including texts, passwords, photos, *and* more **can end up in the wrong hands**

1 IN 10

people have **had an ex that threatened to post nude pictures of them** online

we love to share **50%** of people **like to show their partner their sexy side** with photos or video

 53% of men share intimate media **vs.** **43%** women

 More than **50%** *of* people **share passwords with their partner**

32% of people have **asked** their ex **to delete intimate messages** *and* **pictures**

More people check on their exes' social media accounts than their current partners'

 84% of people have changed passwords after a break up

Digital Romance //
In a Relationship? #CoupleName

P eople put everything online now, including their relationships. It's likely even your first date will end up as an Instagram post. As cute as your new squeeze is, you don't want to jump the gun on making them a part of your online life, which is becoming more permanent than ever.

#inLUV4ever

@Me and @You.

Everyone's social media use is different. Some see it as a throwaway thing they use once in a while, others see it as part of real life interaction. If you and your partner have different ideas about what you should be posting about each other, listen to each other and find a compromise.

The status.

If you want to be "Facebook official" (or whatever other network) make sure it's a mutual thing. No one wants to be pressured into sharing their private life. Wait until you've been dating a while and have introduced each other to your friends and become public in real life.

Reel it in, stalky pants.

Don't obsess over your new love's exes (yes, your selfie is totally better, but stop) or their "likes." The drawback of being connected all the time is that every post and pic is open to over-analysis and misunderstanding.

Offline time.

This goes for friends too, but make sure to spend some quality time with your significant other. Especially when you're just starting to date.

No comparing.

People tend to post the best version of their life online, including their relationships. Don't get discouraged scrolling through your best friend's 500-photo engagement album when things are less than blissful with your partner. Everyone struggles.

Brag—a little.

Take it slow, but it's okay to show online that you and your honey are happy together, if you're into that. Overdoing it will seem insincere, though.

Keep social media where it belongs – at the bottom of your priorities when it comes to dating and relationships. It's okay to peek at a new date's posts to make sure they're not nuts, but don't use it as your sole measure of them or your relationship.

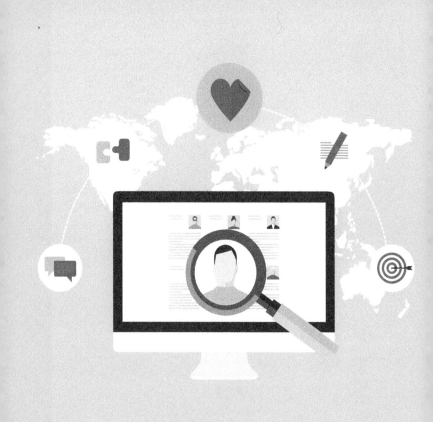

**Digital Romance //
So I Creep, Yeaaah**

Are you allowed to snoop in a relationship? With everyone you know (and don't want to know) available at the click of a button, sometimes paranoia stops by for a visit. Apart from social media, public records are readily searchable online. It's way too easy to jump down the rabbit hole of trying to figure out the "truth" about someone, and not always healthy.

Background Checks?

Public records were once the domain of journalists and lawyers, but now pretty much anyone can go online and look up your five DUI arrests and that time you punched a guy at a football game. He said the Miami Dolphins sucked, and it hurt because it was a little true. You were just being sincere.

This topic is sort of up in the air. You should definitely know what's online about you. But should you do a background check in a new relationship? Usually, if you have mutual friends, you could ask around and get their story. With online dating in the mix, you can be meeting a complete stranger. If you do search, keep it to the mini-mum—crime. And don't bring up anything you find unless it's a huge red flag, like domestic violence.

Trusting No One

Once you're in a relationship, privacy and trust issues come into play. Here's how to get through the thorny questions:

Talk it out.

It's best early on to establish boundaries. Is a little snooping okay or expected? Are both of your phones on lockdown, only to be peeled from your cold, dead hands? Try to find a compromise to avoid fighting later.

Why snoop?

Does your partner seem untrustworthy? What's your evidence? It's better to talk about your misgivings than sneaking a peek at their phone.

My phone's dead, babe.

Can you use their devices once in a while? If they won't let you near their computer, that's not a good sign. Trust is a two-way street.

It's you, not them.

If you have a strong desire to dig up dirt about your partner or snoop through their online activity—the problem doesn't usually start with them. Re-evaluate your trust issues.

Sketchy behavior.

On the other hand, talk to your partner about things that could be making you insecure. It could be a lack of communication or affection on their part.

To the couch.

Sometimes we need extra help to get rid of what's holding us back from trusting people. Seek out a therapist if you can, or find someone to talk to.

No pain, no whoopee.

The possibility of pain is inevitable when you're intimate with someone. The only way to not get hurt is to avoid humanity at all costs. It's an option, but maybe go to therapy and face your fears instead. If that sounds unbearable, channel that fear into building your very own apocalyptic bunker.

It's a pop-up, I swear!

Everyone has, uh, private interests. If it's harmless, but will bother your partner, erase your history or use private browsing. (On the other hand, if your partner is militant against porn, check out the "After Hours" section). And don't snoop for what you don't want to find. If you trust them, give them privacy.

Mixing your life with someone else's gets complicated. People have different ideas of what privacy means. Maybe you feel you have nothing to hide, while your partner keeps a few harmless secrets. It's up to you to determine if you want to make a big deal out of it.

**Digital Romance //
Stalking and Harassment**

$\mathbf{S}$ ometimes an online affair—or a simple chat on a dating site—will go terribly wrong. There are some people who can't take no for an answer. With all our information online, it's become easier than ever to keep tabs on someone. To avoid getting tracked, keep these things in mind:

Public or private.

Decide whether to make your online profiles private. If you often share where you are, where you work, and who your friends are, you're making it very easy for someone to find you.

Profile tracker.

You've probably opened three dozen accounts on different websites whenever they've asked you to. Be aware of what information is available for other people to see.

Public records.

Don't ever list both your full name and full birth date (especially the year) on your profiles. If someone has both of those items, it's easy to find documents that may list where you live (even your social security number, if someone screwed up on blotting it out). Voter registration and address sites like Spokeo also list private information.

Cut it off.

If someone is making unwanted advances, cut off communication immediately. Keep evidence of all messages with screenshots and print them out, especially if they have threatening language. Block the stalker and make your accounts private, at least temporarily.

Tell friends and family.

Keeping a stalker secret makes it easier for them to frighten and intimidate you. Always tell a few people you trust so they can help if there's trouble. Don't be embarrassed, it can happen to anyone.

Get the word out.

If the stalker is someone you know, like a co-worker, inform your boss or someone else who is in a position to reprimand them.

Call the cops.

If the stalker has said anything threatening, violent, or that clearly states their intention to harass you, go to the cops. Bring along copies of all your messages. You should be able to get a restraining order if necessary.

Cyber-harassment.

Several states distinguish between stalking and harassment, but offer legal options for both. Harassment is defined as frequent online activity intended to torment an individual, while stalking involves making credible threats of harm.

Revenge porn.

If your former partner or a stalker was intimate and took pictures or video, they may decide to post them online. If they do, various websites like Facebook, Twitter, and Reddit have taken a hard stance on posting sexual content without the subject's consent. There may be legal recourse as well, check if your state has laws against it—it's still a new, developing legal issue.

Anyone can be a victim of stalking, and it can be a harrowing, traumatizing experience. But there's no reason to go through it alone. The U.S. Department of Justice reports that 3.4 million people are victims of stalking every year. Take action and don't be afraid to ask for help.

INTIMATE PARTNER VIOLENCE

They impact all types of people of all races/ethnicities.
Rape, Physical Violence, or Stalking Victimization in Lifetime*

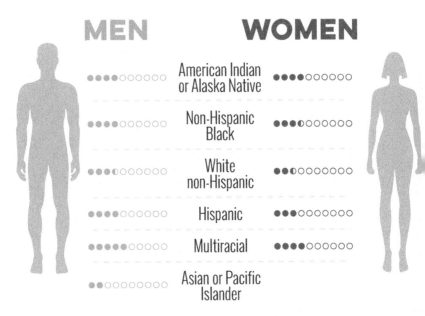

MEN **WOMEN**

MEN		WOMEN
●●●●○○○○○○	American Indian or Alaska Native	●●●●○○○○○○
●●●●○○○○○○	Non-Hispanic Black	●●●◐○○○○○○
●●●◐○○○○○○	White non-Hispanic	●●◐○○○○○○○
●●●●○○○○○○	Hispanic	●●●○○○○○○○
●●●●●○○○○○	Multiracial	●●●●○○○○○○
●●○○○○○○○○	Asian or Pacific Islander	

...varying by income.

Women with a household income less than $**50,000** have a significantly higher prevalence of IPV.

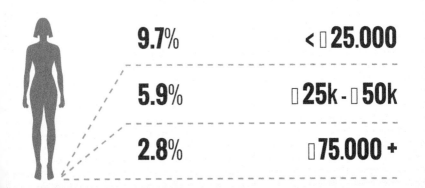

9.7%	< $**25.000**
5.9%	$**25k** - $**50k**
2.8%	$**75.000** +

...impacting people with all sexual orientations

Have been raped in their lifetime

Have experienced sexual violence other than rape in their lifetime.

1 in 2
bisexual women

1 in 2
bisexual men

1 in 8
lesbian women

2 in 5
gay men

1 in 6
heterosexual women

1 in 5
heterosexual men

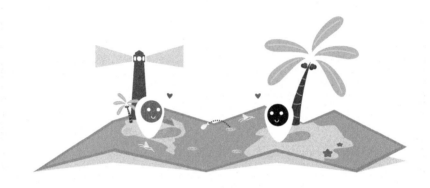

**Digital Romance //
Love You Long Distance**

Sometimes two people meet—whether on vacation, or at school, or some other temporary scenario—and they fall in love! Or infatuation. Or lust. Whatever your bag, it doesn't always have to end like Casablanca. And there isn't a world war going on right now, so have hope.

Faraway Flame

I like you . . . but.

Decide if you really do want to continue seeing this person, or if the fling ends once your plane takes off. If you're thinking about all the dates waiting for you back home, it's for the best to end it.

Tick-tock.

Do you have time for a long distance relationship? Ironically, they're even more time consuming. It takes extra attention to make sure someone feels loved when they can't see you every day.

Dolla bills y'all.

Long distance love is expensive. Flying or driving to another city takes time and money. And once you're there, you're basically on an intense, one-on-one vacation. And yeah, those ain't cheap. Neither are the little gifts you may send to remind your sweetie they're important.

Starting over.

If things are serious, at some point the moving conversation will come up. One of you is going to have to move to the other's city. Or a new city altogether. If that's out of the question, it's best to end it as soon as possible.

Deadlines.

If one of you does want to move, make a concrete timeline. Enduring distance is easier when you know it will end. Plan ahead for graduation or getting a new job.

Trust, but verify.

When you are together, pay attention to things that bother you or may cause arguments. Visits tend to be a romantic whirlwind fueled by desire—but don't let that blind you to your partner's flaws. If you decide to make the big move, those things will only amplify when you see your partner every day.

Love Maintenance

Until the big day arrives when the gap between you and your love is finally closed, you've got to get creative with your dating life. Here are some tips for keeping it going:

Set time aside.

Make time for a nightly call or video chat, if possible. And schedule weekly "dates" where you do something together. Open to interpretation.

Video chat.

It's an obvious one, but Skype will naturally be a staple of your communication. Make sure to give other services a try, like Google Hangouts, which has fun features like drawing on your screen and watching YouTube videos simultaneously.

Video games.

If you're into it, online gaming is a very fun way to go on adventures, even just digitally. A little competition keeps things interesting, and you'll quickly find out if your partner is a sore loser.

Movies.

Movie night is easy to replicate from far away. Sites like Watch2gether, TogetherTube, and InstaSynch will play video for both of you at the same time. You can also do it old school and sync Netflix or a DVD to play at the same time.

Karaoke?

 Yep, there are several websites that let you do karaoke over the internet. Try Karaoke Party for its "battle" feature, and prove to your honey who can serenade best.

Listen to music.

 If you're both busy working on the computer or just tired, try Wavelength or Plug.dj to create a playlist you can listen to together. If you don't want to pick the songs, try 8 Tracks or Live 365 to stream internet radio.

Storytime!

 If you like collaborating or just enjoy writing silly ideas, try Typewrite or Google Docs to write something together.

Touch from afar.

Several apps and physical objects can imitate the feel-ing of touching your love. TapTap, Pillow Talk, and BOND are bracelets that will move or vibrate when touched by your partner's bracelet. Touch Room, Couple, and Intimate are apps that allow you to see your partner touching their phone's screen—you can even share a "Thumbkiss."

Draw!

 Sites like Co Sketch and FlockDraw will allow you to doodle on the same digital whiteboard. The online game Draw It has you guess what the other person is drawing.

Guided tour.

 You can't go out together physically, but there are plenty of digital locations to go to. Google's "Night Walk" is an online guided audio tour through a city of your choice. Some muse-ums, like the Hamilton Civic Museum, have uploaded virtual tours online.

Visits.

Plan to visit each other without straining your budget or personal life. Set clear time frames whenever possible— a visit once every 3 weeks or 2 months, for example. It'll make the wait easier.

Wait, Mr. Postman!

Enough of the digital talk, send something physical once in a while. A handwritten letter or a present is the best thing to find in the mailbox after a long day. Just remember to keep it a surprise, big mouth.

Trust.

The most important thing in a long distance relationship is trusting that the other person won't misbehave. You decide what that means. Some people opt for a "don't ask, don't tell" approach and make exceptions to being monogamous.

Long distance relationships are a temporary solution to a not-so-bad problem: you love somebody, and they're not in the right place. Be attentive, compassionate, and willing to put in a little extra effort before you try.

CHAPTER 3 //
Lovin' and Learnin'

**Lovin' and Learnin' //
Going Steady**

You and your partner are seeing more of each other after a few dates, and maybe you've even become exclusive (or not, we're not judging). How do you start acting like a couple? When do you meet their friends? Here are a few hacks for making this seed flourish into a beautiful something. No need for labels.

First Steps

You're My . . .

Don't rush into the boyfriend/girlfriend/couple labels, unless you want to. If friends ask, you're "seeing someone new" or "dating." And use their name when making introductions, not the awkward "this is my [insert romantic title here]."

Too much love!

In the rush of new love, it's tempting to want to see each other and talk every single second. Take it easy. Absence makes the heart not get tired of having to come up with new, interesting things to say to you every hour.

Clingmaster.

Being loved feels nice, but don't demand it constantly. There's another person at the end of the relationship, and they need to breathe too.

Life happens.

Give each other space to live your lives as usual. Don't cut out friends or skimp on work to focus on your new love. Those are the parts of your life that enrich it (and will still be there if things turn sour).

Hard habits.

When you first meet someone, love makes you a little blind. They seem utterly incapable of doing wrong. Then their little habits and quirks come in, and suddenly they're less than perfect. Address the bad stuff, learn to love their flaws, or say goodbye.

Communication.

 Learn to deal with disagreements and problems early on before they become something bigger and irreconcilable.

L-word.

 Don't necessarily whip out "I love you" too soon or too often. Say it sincerely, and be understanding if the other person isn't quite ready.

Friends.

 Bring friends into the mix slowly. Grab a drink with your date and one or two close friends. The people who know you best will usually give you a solid opinion on a new fling.

Let yourself make mistakes in a new relationship. It doesn't all have to be a 24-hour fairytale. There's a lot of fumbling and miscommunication that happens between two people who don't know each other well yet. Your brain is addicted to a new drug, and it's going to make you obsess and desire and feel a whole lot of feelings all the time.

THIS IS YOUR BODY
IN LOVE

RUNNING INTO THAT SPECIAL SOMEONE

for the first time may seem like a magical moment where stars align and little animated woodland creatures suddenly appear

In reality, love is quite a shock to your body's system.

- -

This is what really happens when your body
FALLS IN LOVE

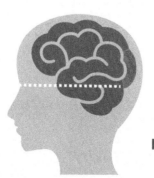

Your eyes meet... From the moment you first see Mr. or Ms. Right, your brain immediately goes into action.

Hubba Hubba! The ventromedial prefrontal cortex judges physical attractiveness in **milliseconds.**

MORE THAN JUST A PRETTY FACE

Your restromedial prefrontal cortex evaluates your love interest from social standpoint and answers the question, "Is this person right for me?"

FOLLOW YOUR NOSE...

Some say pheromones have an effect on human sexual attraction. (They're major players in insect love.)

WHAT A RUSH!

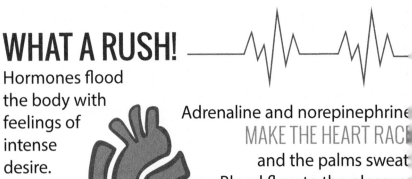

Hormones flood the body with feelings of intense desire.

Adrenaline and norepinephrine MAKE THE HEART RACE and the palms sweat. Blood flow to the pleasure center of the brain increases during the attraction phase leading to an overwhelming fixation on your partner.

I ONLY HAVE EYES FOR YOU

Love lowers levels of the brain chemical
serotonin, which could explain why
lovers display such a single-minded
concentration on the object of
their affection.

BUTTERFLIES IN YOUR STOMACH...

Your body reacts to the stress
of love "rocking your world" by
triggering the brain to release
hormones, which can contract
the blood vessels around your
gut. The loss of blood to that
area causes nausea.

SOMEONE SPECIAL

So if a "meet cute" type situation leaves
you feeling funny, let nature take its course!
That queasiness may mean you found
your soulmate

**Lovin' and Learnin' //
The Little Things**

Use what you're learning about your new partner to develop your bond and show them you're the best friend/lover/foot massager a person could ask for. Making a special effort when you're together will take the pressure off and make you feel more secure.

Be open.

Intimacy comes from sharing yourself with others. You don't have to share every secret, but share the things that make you you. Your fears, hopes, dreams, and that crush you've had on Wolverine since you were a kid.

Be a chef.

You don't have to go to culinary school to cook someone their favorite foods (unless they're really picky). And it's more romantic than Chinese take-out. Again.

Get them a gift.

Don't spend too much, but get them something related to their interests or passions. Bonus points if they've only mentioned that favorite thing once. Either way, it shows you're paying attention.

Make a mixtape.

Okay, I guess it's a playlist now, but at least spring for a CD? Music is always romantic. If you make an actual tape, you get extra retro cred.

Say cheese.

You've probably got a million pictures of each other on your phones. Print a few and frame one. It shows you cherish that time together. Maybe even one of the dog, even if it smells bad most of the time.

Send a sext.

Uh, well, they'll know you're thinking of them?

Drop a note.

Put a short, sweet message somewhere they'll find—a purse, bed, the fridge, wherever.

No homebodies.

If you're the kind of couple that likes to cozy up together at home, make sure not to get into a rut. Make an effort to take your partner somewhere interesting and special. It can be low-key, like an art gallery.

Be yourselves.

The first impressions are over. Let the weirdness hang out and embrace theirs, too. There's nothing better than not holding back with someone.

The most important thing in the early stages of being together is paying attention. You'll build a bond that way. Learn who someone is, and acknowledge them with little acts of kindness that are unique to who they are. Any of the suggestions above can be used whether your partner is feeling up or down, and sometimes it counts the most when it's the latter.

**Lovin' and Learnin' //
Can't Buy Love**

Flying solo means never having to worry about paying for anyone but numero uno. But if you've added a new fling (or a few) into your life, those drink tabs and concert tickets will empty your wallet quickly. You don't want to stay home every night, either. Here are hacks to keep things interesting without being a Scrooge.

Thrifty Adventures

2-for-1 Intoxication.

Don't opt for the trendiest bar that doesn't even have a beer special. Opt for a different, out of the way place where you can talk, shoot a round of pool, and grab a few reasonably-priced drinks. And maybe go out earlier in the week than the standard Saturday night.

Flea or farmers' markets.

Shopping can be a bore, but it's a bit more fun with the quirky and localized touch that these events offer. Try new kinds of food together or see if your sweetie has a hobby you didn't know about. A weird thrifty item or local recipe can be a conversation starter.

Roller or ice skating.

Skating is relatively cheap, it's good exercise, and it's a little dorky. No pressure to look your best or impress with a five-course meal. Just you, your date, some classic rock songs, and a greasy pizza to finish the evening.

Movie night.

No, we don't mean Netflix! Let's get you both out of the house with a revival screening or a midnight movie. Independent theaters sometimes offer free or cheap showings of classic or genre films on the big screen. And websites like Gofobo.com offer free advance screenings of new movies.

Weekend trip.

Find a cool spot in your state within reasonable driving distance, like a national park, a historic town, or a theme park. It'll be as refreshing as a vacation, without the money sucking part.

Contests.

Local newspapers, businesses, and venues are often giving away free tickets to upcoming events. Their social media accounts are the first place to check. Sign up to be a lucky winner!

Music.

For some last minute tunes, look for local shows or check sites like StubHub a few hours before a concert for discounted tickets. And if you're itching to see a big name you love, the app Bandsintown syncs with your music library to give you notifications so you can buy tickets before the scalpers snatch them up and triple the price.

Back to school.

A local college or university will often host concerts, sports games, movie screenings, lectures, and other large events. They're usually open to the public for a reasonable admission fee.

Open mics.

Local venues often host evenings where people can share their music, spoken-word poetry, or stand-up comedy. If you don't mind the unpolished work of fledgling artists, it'll give you both something to think (and talk) about.

'Tis the Season.

If a holiday is coming up, look for a better way to celebrate than an overpriced party. Spend Halloween in a haunted house or hay ride—find one on HauntedHouse.com. Or find a block party to spend New Year's Eve watching free live music and fireworks.

Get your culture on.

Get to know your city! Museums update their collections every few months, or maybe you haven't been to the zoo since you were a kid. Cultural attractions tend to offer free or discounted admission on certain days of the month.

Wild outdoors.

Jump into nature at your local park or beach. Go hiking and observe your local wildlife. The only thing it'll cost you is some snacks and a good pair of shoes. At night, find an observatory or another good stargazing spot for a romantic finish.

Deals, deals, deals.

Sites like Groupon and Restaurants.com will give you a ton of discounts on food, activities, and even vacations. Just be open to trying something new.

Balancing Act

Social butterfly.

Make it clear to your partner how often you like to go out and how much you're willing to spend. No one likes to look like a cheapskate after they've made plans.

Agree on money.

If your date doesn't like how little or how much you like to go out, your lifestyles may be incompatible. Same goes for how much you're spending.

Split the cost.

Once the awkwardness of the first few dates subsides, don't worry as much about picking up the check. It depends on each other's expectations, but typically it's better if each of you pays for things more or less evenly. Maybe they buy concert tickets and you pick up dinner, or they pay for all of it and you pick up the next date's cost. Even if one person is wealthier than the other, it's good to pull your weight in the costs of dating (within your own budget—don't stretch yourself thin).

It's tempting to go out and see the same reliable places and people every weekend, but it's important to try new things when you're just getting to know each other. Getting to see how a person reacts to different situations is a fundamental way to decide if you fit together as a couple. Of course, you don't want to spend a fortune on the trials of this love odyssey.

**Lovin' and Learnin' //
After Hours**

t's likely you want to get to know your partner all sorts of ways, but there's a lot you can do to make sex more fun, personal, and enjoyable. Don't just go with whatever you've always done. Each person is new, uncharted territory, and so are their interests, preferences, and kinks. You may learn a few new things about yourself, too.

Not So Fast

Safety.

The number one thing you should always care about is staying healthy in bed. And not just avoiding pregnancy. Remember that there are lots of STDs and STIs waiting to crawl into your junk (yeah, gross, we know). Condoms are the staple, but check out sites like Planned Parenthood and Scarleteen for more options and things to consider.

Get tested.

No matter how much you like and trust your new love, get tested. Go together so it doesn't come off as accusatory. If they don't want to or they don't like to use protection, they may not have your best interests at heart.

Figure out what you like.

There's a whole Internet out there for you to explore. See what rocks your boat, so to speak. Don't make someone guess how to do it.

The question.

Your first sexual rendezvous may likely be the frantic oh-my-god-you're-so-attractive variety, but at some point you should ask, "What are you into?" Open up about what you both like in bed and what works for you.

Don't forget.

Well, the first question should really be, "Do you want to have sex?" Maybe not stated like Siri, but be absolutely sure you have the consent of your partner before getting into anything. Especially if any kind of alcohol or drugs are involved.

Consent isn't comfort.

Sometimes people can say "yes," when they really mean they don't want to do everything you want to do. They may just want to kiss and fool around under your shirt a bit and call it a night. Be attentive and kind to your partner before, during, and after sex.

Fumble, fumble.

Sex can be awkward with a new person, because you're getting to know how their body works. Humans all have the same parts, but there's infinite variety in what they find pleasurable.

Show and tell.

You and your partner's kinks and preferences should become part of your evening repertoire. If there's something one of you doesn't understand or that's new to you, talk about it. Always be clear.

Safety.

Yep, again. Some kinks can be dangerous, especially those that involve pain. *50 Shades of Grey* glossed over this part, but safely bringing some pain-inducing tricks into the bedroom requires research and ponying up cash for supplies made from good-quality materials. And it's necessary to educate your partner. If it sounds boring, wear a sexy researcher costume while you Google a tutorial.

Porn.

It's a touchy issue, but judging by the booming porn industry, someone's watching that stuff. And it may be you. Be upfront with your partner if it's something you enjoy. If they're disgusted or infuriated by it, consider whether or not you want to erase your browser history forever.

Good, giving, and game.

The popular slogan of sex columnist Dan Savage, being "GGG" means being open to trying new things in bed, while always being aware of your wishes and needs, and those of your partner. It's great advice not just for the bedroom, but for keeping your relationship open and fun.

That's about it for getting the sex train rolling. For everything else, you have the internet—just pick the right resources. Generally professional columnists and educational sites (like the ones mentioned above) are a good bet. Avoid random forums and the like. There are a lot of people with skewed ideas about how sex and relationships work. Make sure both your partners and your sources fit your values. Opposites attract, but not when it comes to sex. Someone who isn't into your lifestyle isn't going to stick around in the long term.

Lovin' and Learnin' //
So Happy (Living) Together

It's typically the step that some take when things are going well and you can't stand the idea of waking up every morning without your better half by your side. But are you ready? Is it a necessary step? Who's going to do the dishes? Living together brings a lot of unsexy—but important—questions into the mix.

Can I Come Over . . . Forever?

You loooooove each other.

Everything is going really well. Like, all your friends are tired of hearing you talk about how much fun you have together, how cute your sweetie is when they sleep, how adorable your adopted Shih Tzus are and how—we get it, just shut up already.

You're over all the time.

If you're pretty much living together and leaving an empty apartment to collect cobwebs, may as well save on the rent, right? Just be aware that there's nowhere to go except the couch (or a hotel) when a big fight happens.

Big grown-up summit.

You've already discussed the possibility of a long-term relationship, you both do or don't want kids, and the idea of settling into an eco-friendly brownstone in a multicultural neighborhood with a nice dog park doesn't repulse you.

The little things.

Don't jump into it. If your partner's snoring is unbearable or their idea of cleanliness is shoving things in the closet, you should address that first.

It's mutual.

If there's even the slightest doubt in your mind about whether you'd like to live with them—or vice versa—definitely don't do it. Living together is the first major step to committing to someone, so don't take it lightly.

Vacation survival.

You've survived a vacation or some other situation where you had to live together (extra points for a family holiday) and deal with new, stressful, and frustrating things. If you made it out alive, you may be suited to sharing a place.

Ew, people.

If one of you likes constant visitors, while the other likes absolute silence unless they step out the front door, your lifestyles may not be compatible. This applies to other little things, too—what time you cook dinner, if you smoke, and how early you wake up in the morning.

What's That Smell?

Brand new place!

You've decided to live together, said adios to the roommate, but what now? Well, it's time to talk. A lot. About everything.

Finances.

It's easy enough to split the rent or the electric bill. But who's buying groceries? Who pays the vet bills? If you can't afford the plumber, will you pay your partner back? Be open about finances so one person doesn't feel like they're paying for everything.

Cleaning.

You are two disgusting animals sharing the same cage (you have great taste in furniture, though). Someone's gotta clean it. Cleaning takes time and energy, so split up your duties evenly. It's okay to not share each thing evenly, however. If one person is better at cleaning the floor, and the other prefers cleaning the bathroom, that's a good compromise.

Don't get too cozy.

You may have a tendency to become couch potatoes when living together, ordering take-out and watching movies all day. Don't enable each other's bad habits. Stay healthy by cooking at home and working out more.

TMI all the time.

You will become intimately familiar with the smells, sounds, and sights of your partner when they haven't spruced up just for you. You don't have to poop with the door open, but hopefully your partner will be only politely horrified by the smell coming from the bathroom.

Spend time apart.

When you live together, your partner will get a bit closer to being the center of your life—they're in your house, after all. Avoid getting sick of each other by making time for friends, hobbies, and other fun non-relationship stuff.

Living together is the next step for a couple in love, so both parties should be clear about each other's intentions. It sends the message to your partner and everyone else that marriage or another long-term commitment may be in store. That's not a requirement—so be clear about what it means to you. And for practical purposes, be open about what you want from your new roommate. Don't be shy about asking them to take out the trash just because you like to make out with them.

Lovin' and Learnin' //
Getting Down After 5

Your dating life is going to take up a lot of energy and time, especially if you're successful in finding someone who likes to see you for more than an hour. To balance the jumble of work, life, play, basic hygiene, and staring-at-the-ceiling time you're gonna need some hacks. Here are a few to make sense of your messy life.

While Exploring

Don't over-prioritize.

Give your dating life some attention, but don't mindlessly click through OkCupid for hours. Limit the amount of time to a reasonable amount, maybe half an hour every other day. And make that time decisive: message some potential dates or finalize a date with someone.

Ignore the stats.

Don't spend time or energy wondering why people reject you. They've simply got their own interests, goals, and needs, same as you do.

Don't go overboard.

Make sure your social life doesn't only consist of failed and lukewarm dates, or you're bound to get into a rut. Go out with friends and take the pressure off for a night.

Out of sight.

As exciting as it might be to get messages, send the notifications to a separate email address or folder. Be decisive and delete messages from people you're not 100% interested in.

Message-mania.

If someone has a habit of sending multiple messages in a day before you even respond to the first one, nip that relationship bud before it starts. Unless you enjoy constant "wut r u up 2?" texts.

Keep light goals.

Be honest with yourself about what you want. Do you want a relationship? That's okay. A lot of people do. Take that into consideration when picking dates that may not fit that need.

Relationship In-Progress

Set boundaries.

Once someone important is in your life, it's necessary to give them the time and love they need. It's up to both of you to decide what that means. If you're constantly thinking about work, learn to leave it at the office. Make a separate inbox for work emails and turn off the notifications so you can only check it during work hours. It's okay to work a few late nights, but not every night.

Schedule time.

It seems a little robotic to set aside certain hours or evenings aside for romance, but love isn't always about spontaneity. Sometimes it's enough to make your partner feel special. Make a date night that can't be rescheduled or plan to always have dinner together.

Apps to the rescue.

When you're apart, use an app like Couple to send private messages, thumb kisses, doodles, or maybe a link to share something cool you read online.

Up-to-date.

Check in with your partner, especially during that one-on-one time. Ask them if they're happy and are getting everything they need. And express your feelings, too.

Work selectively.

Every day of your career isn't going to be the big, turning-point day. Prioritize work when you know it'll count most—for a big project or before a possible promotion.

Quality, not quantity.

 Love doesn't always require staring into each other's eyes for hours. A small kindness every day can really make a difference in the long run.

In a culture that values practicality over all things, you may be inclined to worry where your time is best spent. No one likes to invest in something that fails. But having genuine, sincere relationships with others—even just for an evening—increases your empathy, your understanding of yourself, and if nothing else maybe you learn another trick for the bedroom. Your very thorough marketing plan isn't making anyone swoon, so don't give it more attention than necessary. Half of the people who see it will just be thinking about sex anyway. Or ice cream. Or both.

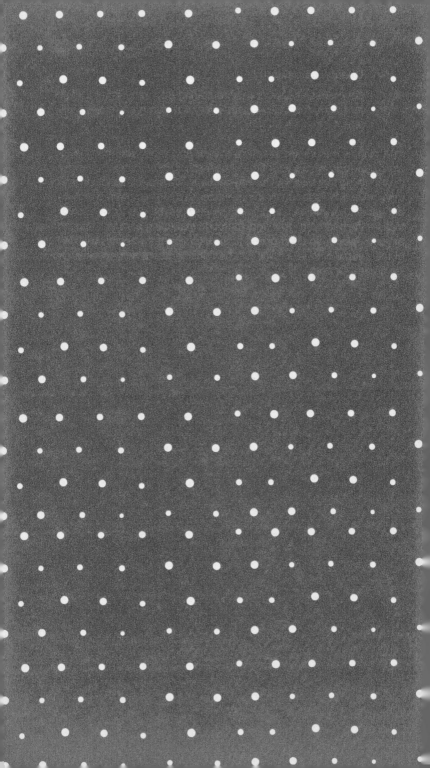

CHAPTER 4 //
Tough Love

**Tough Love //
Frenemies**

A t some point your date may become more than someone you awkwardly say goodbye to the morning after an evening of debauchery. Once things are going well, you'll want them to meet your friends and family. You can keep them a secret forever, but that's really complicated. Let's take the easier route.

Friends Forever

Introductions.

Ideally at least one of your friends has heard of or talked to your new lover—it's good to get a second opinion. If things are going well after several dates, take them out to hang out with your gang.

Prep talk.

Tell your date about your friends beforehand, so they're not totally confused when they meet them. Mention common interests they might share.

First steps.

Introduce your date and initiate some conversation with your friends. Don't do all the talking, let your date speak for themselves. If they're shy, try to bring up things that might get them talking.

Keep up.

Don't neglect your date so they're awkwardly sitting alone. And if you're the one being introduced, don't expect to automatically fit in with the group. Make an effort to get to know everyone.

Ask questions.

If you're meeting your date's friends, ask them about their interests, lives, and fun stories about your date. People love to talk about themselves.

Woops.

If it doesn't go well, don't give up right away. First impressions aren't the only impressions. But if your friends have strong, legitimate opinions about your date—they don't like how you're being treated, for instance—hear them out.

Like!

If things go well, wait a bit and add one or two friends that you liked best on whatever social network you use. It's a small gesture, but a nice one.

Pass.

If you don't like your date's friends at all (not even one), you'll have to take into account that they're part of his or her social life. You'll have to see them at some point. If that's unbearable, you may want to reconsider the relationship. Even if you're honest with your partner about their friends, it's probably not going to go well.

Your Other Loved Ones

Time it right.

Don't make meeting your family a nerve-wracking experience for your partner. Make sure they're okay with it and try to start small—introduce them to a sibling first.

Right location.

It might be good to get out on a family date rather than go for the typical dinner. Everyone will have something fun and new to talk about while they get to know each other.

Presents!

If you're the one meeting the family, bring a small gift like a bottle of wine or a dessert (if you're having dinner). This is America, we win love with food and material objects. Don't overdo it and spend a ton, though.

It's boring.

Depending on your parents' personalities and comfort level, the conversation isn't going to extend far beyond the standard "what do you do" and "what are your plans for the future." Boring is fine, everyone will be pleased.

Keep it safe.

Unless you enjoy throwing Molotov cocktails onto the dinner table, stay away from the standard firecracker subjects—politics, religion, or sex. Stay milquetoast and ask nice questions to nice people. Talk, but don't talk too much.

Be interesting.

Don't be too boring, either. Feel free to talk about your super special study abroad trip, for instance. Make sure to share all the lovely things that someone who read Eat, Pray, Love would like to hear.

Awkward is temporary.

Hopefully, you or your date will hit it off with the parents, and things will get less dull and uncomfortable over time. Maybe they'll even offer you drugs (we can dream).

Awkward is forever.

On the other hand, the closer you get, the more you'll become privy to all the family secrets, quirks, and less-than-polite behavior.

Tolerable.

Realize that if you stick around with your partner, their family becomes your family. If you really can't stand them, it could be a deal breaker.

It ain't easy to meet all the people who have history with your new love. It's a little intimidating considering the influence they may have over them. And whether or not you think it's legitimate, their opinions can make or break the relationship. In the long run you can't fake who you are, and you shouldn't have to. Making those first few meetings as friendly and non-confrontational as possible can pave the way for you to feel more comfortable being yourself. Unless you don't care, in which case do you, dude. Full steam ahead.

9 WAYS TO
IMPROVE YOUR RELATIONSHIP

WHAT DOESN'T KILL YOU
A little stress early on in relationships builds resilience for the road.

1

2 ### DON'T BE A NAG
Change yourself; don't try to change your partner.

ALL SALES FINAL!
Product Sold as is

PHONE IT IN
People who call their partners more report more love and commitment.
(A text isn't a call)

3

4 ### BE NICE
People whose partners are dismissive have faster heart rates and feel worse after a stressful task.

WORK IT OUT
Talking always helps, so don't be afraid to speak up, even if you fell stuck in the relationship.

5

6 HAVE REALISTIC EXPECTATIONS

People seldom change, and you'll only get frustrated if you expect them to do so.

7 TALK OPENLY ABOUT SEX

Communicating about sex is linked to greater relationship satisfaction, especially for couples who have been together longer.

8 CUDDLING SIGNIFICANTLY IMPROVES SEXUAL AND RELATIONSHIP SATISFACTION

12: The number of minutes they reported talking intimately after sex

26: The number of minutes participants reported "cuddling, caressing and spooning after sex"

10: The number of minutes they reported kissing after sex

9 COUPLES WITH AN ACTIVE FACEBOOK PRESENCE PERCEIVED BY OTHERS TO HAVE BETTER RELATIONSHIPS

25% of couples have a picture of two people (i.e.. them and their partner)

70% of couples have an "In Relationship" status on Facebook and are perceived by others to have better relationships

Tough Love //
Opinionator

It's pretty much a given that you're going to have different opinions than your partner, even if you're so similar and get along so well (ohmigerd ??? soulmates). And why wouldn't you want that? Who wants to agree all the time? Even if your fights are mostly over doing laundry, it can foster growth. Here are some hacks on how to argue without calling it quits every time.

Acceptable Arguing

Setting.

The best place to talk about a difficult topic is either over food or at least in-person. Avoid texting or phone calls—you're more likely to misinterpret tone or hang up dramatically. In-person, you have the benefit of a hug or kiss to diffuse the situation.

Don't fight angry.

Seems counterintuitive, but the best time to settle your differences is after the initial rage has passed. Once that happens, don't let the problem go—it'll just build up resentment. Discuss what's bothering you calmly.

You did this/that.

Keep "you" out of your statements to your partner. It sounds accusatory. Preface your statements with "I feel that."

Passive aggressive.

Don't say "it's fine" when it's not fine. Be honest if you're mad because your partner did something that frustrates you. They may not even realize anything is wrong unless you tell them.

Spread positivity.

Be calm and assure your partner you want to get something out of the argument. Your goal should never be to win the fight, but mutual growth (we know you're right, but that's not the point).

The other side.

Consider your partner's points, don't just shut them down. You both feel and think differently, and the idea is to come to an understanding. And that applies to every part of your life, not just romance.

Ask questions.

You may be speaking the same language, but not understanding each other at all. Always ask questions to clarify.

Stalemate.

Some fights are never settled, but they aren't deal breakers. Some things will always bother you about your partner. It's okay. As long as you recognize the conflict and can laugh it off over time, it can work out.

End the fight.

If you can come to an understanding, come up with ways to communicate better or to treat the person better in the future (depending on what the fight was about). If you can't end on a good note, take a break and address it later. Sleep on it or talk to someone you trust about your issues.

Political feud.

Whether or not this one matters to you is your choice (you might see where we're going with this). Some people like a good debate and others would rather everyone shut up and be nice. And not all political and social issues are created equally; tax reform is a lot less personal than, say, abortion. If you're of the mind that the latter is a basic right, well, it's probably a deal breaker if your partner doesn't agree. It really depends if you're emotionally invested in your positions.

The tough questions.

You should really get moral and worldview questions out of the way as soon as possible. This sounds abstract, but it's really not. Whether or not someone will throw a dollar to a homeless person, if they like traveling and exploring new cultures, or their religious beliefs, for instance, are all important tidbits that make up a person. It may not be important now when it's all cuddly and fun, but 20 years down the line you'll want to visit Thailand and they'll want to stay home.

A lot of couples are afraid of disagreements, but it's actually best to tackle them head on as soon as they come up. Don't let a molehill turn into a mountain (we think that's the saying, anyway). Even if you fight often, how you end those arguments matters more than whether or not you have them. And above all, it depends on how much energy you're willing to put into the relationship.

DATING DEAL BREAKERS

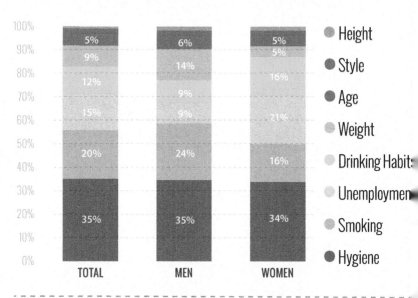

- Height
- Style
- Age
- Weight
- Drinking Habits
- Unemployment
- Smoking
- Hygiene

TOTAL
- 5%
- 9%
- 12%
- 15%
- 20%
- 35%

MEN
- 6%
- 14%
- 9%
- 9%
- 24%
- 35%

WOMEN
- 5%
- 5%
- 16%
- 21%
- 16%
- 34%

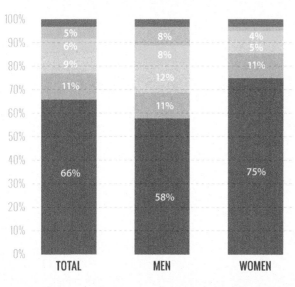

- Don't like your favorite team
- Don't go to the gym
- Different taste music
- Prefer different foods
- Different politics
- Don't get along with your friends

TOTAL
- 5%
- 6%
- 9%
- 11%
- 66%

MEN
- 8%
- 8%
- 12%
- 11%
- 58%

WOMEN
- 4%
- 5%
- 11%
- 75%

Tough Love //
That Jealousy Bug

It's the great disease of any relationship, and can often be a death knell for it. Jealousy eats away at an otherwise healthy relationship. The fear that someone might come along and snag your sweetheart probably isn't helped by the fact that anyone either of you has ever known is just a click away. But just because something can happen, doesn't mean it will. Here's how to fight that negative tug at your hearts.

Beat It

Define it.

How is jealousy coming up in your relationship? Is one of you always worried that the other is going to cheat, so you're constantly checking where your partner is? Are you or your partner throwing a fit if they so much as look at someone good-looking? Are you upset that your partner is liking posts of attractive acquaintances online?

Talk it out.

Sincerely address what's making you or your partner feel jealous. Don't call them crazy or irrational—confrontation won't solve the issue. Jealousy is a normal, common emotion that becomes a problem only when people wallow in it or blow it out of proportion rather than letting it pass.

Self-evaluate.

There can be any number of reasons why someone feels jealous: an unfaithful ex, family relationships, anxiety or mood disorders, or any experience that makes it difficult to trust others. Be compassionate to a partner who may feel this way, but advise them to seek out professional help if they can't address it on their own.

"I saw you do that."

If it's the result of miscommunication or an innocent gesture taken the wrong way, look for ways to communicate better in the future.

Take time apart.

Jealousy can form when partners spend too much time to-gether or become too dependent on each other to feel good about themselves. Find other people and activities that sup-port your self-esteem and well-being.

Greener grass.

Stop comparing yourself to others. Your partner is with you for a reason, and no one thinks about your flaws as much as you do.

Draw the line.

To fix jealousy, it's helpful to understand the boundaries of your relationship. Is your partner okay if you're friendly, or even a little flirtatious, when you're out at a party or event? What does your partner need from you to feel secure? Is talking to or being friends with exes okay? Is checking out someone attractive allowed?

Zero-tolerance.

Jealousy has no place in a long-term relationship (or really any). If someone is repeating their jealous behavior even af-ter it's been addressed, it may be time to end things.

We often feel that by partnering up with someone, we're entitled to know every little thing about them. The truth is that we never really know. At some point you have to believe that if someone is dedi-cating their time and love to you, they mean it. That doesn't mean ignoring red flags. But do you really want to live your life questioning everyone who's nice to you?

**Tough Love //
Spotting Abuse**

Things may be going well with you and your new honey, but maybe you're having doubts. Something rubs you the wrong way about them. They blew up at you that one time you were late to dinner, or they criticize the way you dress. It seems hard to believe that your perfect-on-paper partner could be labeled "abusive," but sometimes the little negative tics add up to something serious. Here are a few ways to figure out if your partner may be slowly chipping away at your well-being.

Abuser Scorecard

Criticism.

Everyone's a critic, but constant criticism is a sign that someone genuinely doesn't like you, is projecting their insecurities, or is trying to knock your self-esteem.

Unwelcome opinions.

An abuser may try to control what you wear and how you look. They may be uncomfortable with you being sexy or talking to attractive people.

X-treme jealousy.

We addressed run-of-the-mill jealousy earlier, but an abusive partner will take more extreme measures to keep you in check. Monopolizing your time, demanding to know your whereabouts at all times, and keeping you away from friends and family are all signs of a controlling partner.

I love you, but.

It's a common trap to frame criticism or demands as a flaw that they're dealing with for your sake. Don't be convinced that love requires meeting someone's needs without considering your own.

Unpredictable.

If you're partner's mood swings or bouts of anger have you walking on eggshells, it's not healthy. A partner should be reliable and communicative about what they need. An abusive partner will have moody outbursts when you've done nothing wrong.

Shutting down.

A partner can be emotionally abusive without yelling. Sometimes ignoring you, clamming up, or excluding you from their life is enough to make you feel horrible—and they know it. Don't fall for the silent treatment.

I'm just joking.

A sense of humor is good for any relationship, humans are weird. But someone who mocks you, especially in front of others, is as bad as a playground bully. Even if they claim they're "only kidding."

Guilt trips.

Bringing up your previous mistakes, inventing slights, or making you feel bad about your past are all ways an abuser stays in control. By making you feel inferior, they gain the advantage. This makes you open to ridiculous demands—like never seeing friends who they see as competition.

Unwanted contact.

Physical abuse doesn't have to look like a black eye. An abuser may scratch, punch, bite, kick or throw things at you. They may grab your face to make you pay attention to them. It may not leave a mark, but anyone who touches you without permission is violating you.

Coerced or forced sex.

Just because you're dating someone doesn't give them automatic access to your body. Guilt tripping you into sex or forcing you to say yes is assault. If you've been raped, get away from your partner and call the police. See our "Tough Stuff" section for more advice.

Physical violence.

Get away from someone who resorts to breaking or punching things to express their feelings. It's unacceptable behavior. They may be punching a wall today, but tomorrow it could be you.

Threatening suicide.

Any decent human being is going to worry about someone who says they'll commit suicide. But if it's accompanied by the behavior we've outlined above, it's likely to be another ploy to keep you around. It's impossible to know when a suicide threat is real, so always call 9-1-1 and get the person out of your life as soon as possible. You're not responsible for their self-harm.

Resources for Abuse

9-1-1-- Contact police if someone is being violent with you or you feel that you can't get away from them safely.

The National Domestic Violence Hotline -- 1-800-799-7233
Contact them 24/7 to speak to someone about your abuser, how to deal with them, or even if you're having doubts about whether your relationship is healthy.

The National Teen Dating Abuse Helpline – 1-866-331-9474
The helpline is available online (loveisrespect.org) via chat and via text message as well. Contact them for help with unhealthy and abusive relationships and figure out your next steps.

The National Suicide Prevention Lifeline – 1-800-273-8255
If you feel hopeless about your relationship and are considering suicide, call for help 24/7.

Friends & Family -- Don't let an abuser keep you away from the people who love you most. They're the first people you should tell when the signs of abuse crop up.

Therapy/Counseling -- If things haven't progressed to the worst stages, a therapist or counselor will help you identify the unhealthy aspects of your relationship. If you're in college, counseling is likely available for free.

It's not easy to end any relationship, even an abusive one. The emotional effects of abuse, especially the hit to your self-esteem, will linger even after the abuser is long gone. It's hard to even label a former partner as an "abuser"—it seems melodramatic. Don't be ashamed, if the shoe fits, that's what they are. And they don't deserve you.

KNOW THE 8
BEFORE IT'S TOO LATE

INTENSITY

Excessive charm, LYING to cover up inssecurity, needing to win over your friends and family immediately, OVER THE TOP gestures that seem too much too soon, BOMBARDING you with numerous texts and emails in a short time, behaving obsessively, insisting that you get serious IMMEDIATELY.

JEALOUSY

Responding IRRATIONALLY when you interact with other people, becoming ANGRY when you speak with th opposite sex, persistently ACCUSING you of flirting/cheating, resenting your time with friends and family or DEMANDING to kno private details of your life.

CONTROL

TELLING how to wear your hair, when to speak or what to think, showing up UNINVITED at your home/school/job, CHECKING your cell phone, emails, Facebook, going through your belongings, following you, sexually coercing you or making you FEEL BAD about yourself.

ISOLATION

INSISTING you only spend time with him or her, making you emotionally or psychologically DEPENDENT preventing you from seen your family or friends, or fror going to school or work.

CRITICISM

Calling you overweight, UGLY, STUPID or crazy, ridiculing your beliefs, ambitions or friends, telling you he or she is the only one who really cares about you. BRAINWASHING you to feel worthless.

SABOTAGE

Making you MISS work, school, an interview, test or competition by getting sick, breaking up with you or HIDING your keys, wallet, text books or phone, STEALING your belongings.

BLAME

Making you feel GUILTY and responsible for his or her behavior, blaming the world or you for his or her PROBLEMS, emotional manipulation, always saying "this is your FAULT"

ANGER

OVERREACTING to small problems, frequently losing control, violent OUTBURSTS, having severe mood swings, drinking or partying excessively when upset, making THREATS, picking FIGHTS, having a history of violent beehavior and making you feel AFRAID.

Tough Love //
The Hard Stuff

Ve hope your dating life is full of fun experiences and nothing more unpleasant than a date that just dragged on for too long (we know that one guy with the $400 pen that writes "so smooth" was awful). But the worst can happen, and no one should head out into the dating world without knowing what to do.

Unwanted Pregnancy

It's the big worry of anyone with a uterus, and sometimes birth control and condoms don't do the trick. Or you made a genuine mistake and forgot to use either. We're all human. About half of all U.S. women will have an unplanned pregnancy. When you're not in a committed relationship, though, it can add more stress to an already difficult decision.

Decide whether to share.

Your body, your choice. It also depends on the relationship. You don't have to tell the person you're dating if you choose to terminate the pregnancy. But if you see a future with them, and you want this person to be someone you trust, it may be good to share. Do tell if you plan to keep the baby, unless you feel your partner would harm either of you.

Going through with the pregnancy.

Having a child is no easy choice, and it may not be an emotionally or financially viable decision for some. You also should take into account if you'll be parenting alone or if your partner will decide to be involved. Many people choose single-parenting or co-parenting. There's no foolproof answer.

Adoption.

If you don't want to have an abortion and don't want to or can't become a parent, adoption is the in-between. You have two options, either a closed or open adoption. "Closed" means the adopting family and the child will be given no information about you. "Open" means you can choose the family and remain in contact with them.

Abortion.

Terminating your pregnancy is a personal decision and should be determined by you alone. If you feel that you're not interested in being pregnant at this point in your life, that's fine. There are several different methods and you should ask your doctor questions about each. Keep in mind that earlier is better—it's an easier process at 3 months than at 6 or 9 months. Most states have restrictions on abortions after 18-20 weeks of pregnancy. If you have concerns, get a thorough gynecological exam and ask your doctor about the process. If you are normal and healthy, it should be a safe procedure.

Resources

Planned Parenthood - http://www.plannedparenthood.org/

They're the most famous name in sexual health and women's health, and it's for a reason. Your local clinic will guide you through every step of deciding what to do about your pregnancy and will respect your private information if you're a legal adult (some states require parental consent for teens). If you choose to have an abortion, it can be done in-clinic or you'll be referred to another doctor.

Adoption.com - http://adoption.com/

If you're wondering how to get started in the adoption process, Adoption.com is a great first resource on the subject. There are also tons of forums so you can explore others' questions or ask your own.

USDA – Women, Infants, and Children (WIC) - http://www.fns.usda.gov/wic/women-infants-and-children-wic

If you're deciding to become a parent, you will otherwise go through the normal process of a pregnancy. But if you feel you'll struggle financially with the costs of a pregnancy, giving birth, and raising a child, start with the WIC program. The Special Supplemental Nutrition Program for Women, Infants, and Children gives grants to states to provide resources on nutrition to low-income pregnant women.

No matter what you decide to do, talk to a close friend or family member about the situation. Have someone by your side if your partner isn't willing to be there. It's hard enough to be pregnant when you don't want to be, but you don't have to do it alone.

Sexually Transmitted Diseases

Sex always comes with the risk of disease, even when you use pro-tection. If you find yourself not feeling great down there, go to your doctor or STD clinic as soon as possible. Don't be embarrassed, it happens to a lot of people, and probably has to a few of your friends and family (we know, gross, but your parents are people too). Your doctor has seen much worse and only cares about your health.

Keep in mind that many diseases are asymptomatic. Make it a point to get tested regularly if you have an active sex life (even just one partner). How frequently depends on how many sexual partners you have, but at a minimum once a year is recommended. And in the meantime, use protection. Don't fall for any complaints on that front. Show the door to anyone who balks at a condom—they don't respect your health.

Sexual Assault and Rape

As we mentioned earlier, even someone you know can abuse your trust and violate your boundaries. If anyone has touched you, ha-rassed you, or forced you to have sexual contact you didn't want (not just intercourse), you'll want to get help immediately.

Rape is not your fault. There is no foolproof way to prevent rape, no matter what you wear or how much pepper spray you carry in your purse. Don't let anyone pin the blame for your assault on you—it's always the fault of the rapist.

If you are raped or assaulted:

Get to a safe place.If you want to report the crime, call police immediately. There's no guarantee that they will be sensitive or kind about it, but they are obligated to listen to you and collect evidence of the crime.

If you are reporting the crime, keep all physical evidence of the assault, especially clothes. Place them in paper bags. Do not shower or clean yourself or the area where the rape occurred.

Call someone you trust to help you through reporting the crime, going to the hospital, or just talking about the crime.

Get to an emergency room so they can conduct a physical exam. Ask for a urine test to check if you were given a date rape drug.

If you're confused or don't want to report the crime, call the rape crisis hotline below. They'll listen to you and give you options.

It's likely you will need counseling to recover from the assault. If you don't know where to find help, contact the RAINN hotline below.

If you're not sure if you were raped:

If you feel confused about whether your sexual encounter was consensual, still go through as many of the steps above as you feel comfortable doing. Just because you didn't resist, didn't say no, or were intoxicated doesn't mean you weren't raped. If you were unconscious but you chose to drink, for example—it is still rape.

If you don't feel you were raped, but feel uncomfortable or traumatized after a sexual encounter, talk to someone you trust or call the hotline to talk about what happened. It is absolutely legitimate to not feel good about a sexual experience even though you may have said "yes."

Resources

9-1-1
Contact police to report your assault or rape.

Rape Crisis Hotline – 1-800-656-4673 or **online.RAINN.org**
Call the hotline to talk to a trained staff member about your situation. You will get confidential, judgment-free support to talk about what happened and what you should do next.

RAINN (Rape, Abuse & Incest National Network) –
http://www.rainn.org
As well as being the source of the crisis hotline, they offer a lot of information on getting help if you're not ready to talk to someone.

CHAPTER 5 //
The Future Awaits

**The Future Awaits //
Breaking Up**

So the stars have left your eyes and you've got a bad feeling in your gut. The person sitting across from you on your dates isn't who you want to be with for the rest of your life. Or even tomorrow. It's sad, but it happens to nearly everyone. You gotta do what you gotta do. Here's why breaking up may be in your best interest:

The End is Nigh

Doubts.

Doubt is part of every relationship, but if you find yourself asking over and over if the relationship is right, it may be time to admit it's not.

You'd rather be alone.

The pang of loneliness you felt without your partner nearby isn't really as strong anymore. You'd rather be out with friends not just this Friday night, but every Friday night. Forever.

Mistrust.

You don't think your partner is being faithful and maybe a few peeks at their texts have confirmed your suspicions. Or they seem less interested in you in general.

Different goals.

One of you wants to travel the world while the other wants to settle down in a small town and open a bookstore. If you can't make your lives mesh together, it's better to say goodbye.

Growing apart.

People can change at any point in their life, but especially when they're young and figuring things out. Maybe your partner is a workaholic and you want to have a bit more fun. You may be able to grow together and figure out your differences, or it may be more trouble than it's worth.

No future.

Neither of you, or only one of you, is interested in a future together. The topic makes you uncomfortable every time it comes up.

No agreement.

A lot of people can overlook their differences at first when things are hot and heavy, but major differences on political, religious, and social issues will come 'round to bite you when things settle down. At the end of the day, your core values aren't negotiable.

Ready to rumble.

The biggest sign is that you always fight. Over big and small things. Dumb and random things. And moreover, you don't come out of these fights feeling like you've won a small victory for your relationship. There's yelling, name-calling, and maybe even a physical altercation. And that's when you feel like it's time to tap out.

Make the Break

In-person.

Don't be a coward. Texting, emailing, or messaging via Facebook that you want to break up isn't the way to say goodbye to someone who's given you love and time. If it's only been a few dates, you can get away with a phone call. If not, go for the standard "we need to talk" and meet up in a quiet place. Unless that person has been abusive, in which case a quick text before you block them forever should do the trick.

Timing.

You may be chomping at the bit to be free, but be considerate. If someone has a big, stressful event coming up—a school final, an LSAT, or a big job interview—don't screw that up for them. Wait until it's passed to break the bad news, but don't put it off past that point.

Be kind.

Depending on who's initiating the break up, one of you is going to ask why. Be gentle about laying down the facts. Say you "just don't click" rather than "you smell bad and you're bad at sex." You don't want to scar them for life. Avoid the standard "not ready for a relationship" line. Even if it's true, it can give your ex false hope.

Game-plan.

Lay out what happens after the break up. Be direct about it being over and you wanting space and time for yourself. Be clear about not wanting to talk for a while.

Big mouth.

Don't be a jerk and badmouth an ex. Don't spill their secrets to the world, either. Unless your ex is a danger to other potential partners, no one wants their flaws announced to the world.

Breaking up isn't fun for anyone, but you only get one life (probably, we don't know). It's better to go through the pain of ending something that doesn't work than never finding the right relationship that satisfies you.

PREJUDICE AGAINST
SINGLE PEOPLE?

DO PEOPLE RECOGNIZE THIS PREJUDICE?

Only **30**% of single people believed that singles are stigmatize group. **100**% of gay participants and **86**% of African-American participants perceived discrimination against their groups.

HOW DO PEOPLE DESCRIBE MARRIED AND SINGLE INDIVIDUALS?

Mature

Loving   Stable

MARRIED

Happy   Kind

Honest

Self-centered

Unhappy   Immatur

SINGLE

Lonely   Ugly

Independent

WHO WOULD YOU RENT A HOUSE TO?

70%   15%   10%

Married Couple   Single Woman   Single Man

**The Future Awaits //
Post-Breakup Strategy**

133

reak out the ice cream and sad pop songs—it's wallowing time. Just kidding, you need to get the ball rolling again. Whatever you are, old, young, a ganja-lovin' Rastafarian, you're full of life and deserve to embrace all of it. Don't let a break-up keep you moping forever.

Freedom!

Take it easy.

Calling it quits takes a toll on you emotionally. You basically have a category 5 flu right now, including the runny nose. Keep the Kleenex nearby and take a personal day if you need to. Junk food and Netflix are encouraged. Cosmo may want you to go on a 30-day cleanse, but we support 30 days of pizza.

Talk to people.

When you're ready, tell friends and family what happened. Don't go through it alone. They'll get you out of the house or keep you company on lonely days.

But also tell them to shut up.

A lot of things people say after a break-up are unhelpful, like "I always knew he was a jerk. He was so dumb blahblah-blah." They're trying to rile up your bravado, but they might make you feel as though the past few months or years of your life were a huge waste. Be kind, because they love you, but tell them what they're doing.

Spring cleaning.

You don't have to throw away everything related to your part-ner, but it's best to collect all of it, toss it in a box, and not worry about it until you want to throw it out. Little reminders of gifts and photos will open the wounds every time. How much you want to forget, though, depends on how things ended and whether you want to be friends.

Unfriend.

Do some digital cleaning, too. Wipe the phone and the hard drive of your online memories. If you want, block them on social media. Going through pictures of their latest squeeze is not going to make things easier. Back away from the Internet, it just wants to hurt you.

Or be friends.

It is possible to stay friendly with an ex, but it's good to give each other space for a while. The sting of missing them or seeing them with someone new may be just as bad even if the break-up wasn't.

Get a tattoo.

Change something about your appearance. Feeling fresh and new on the outside will ease the transition. You may want to go for the lighter side, like a haircut, or maybe full-blown body modification (go for it, your spine needs more ribbons).

Extra help.

Okay, we know this is like the 47th time we've suggested this, but talking to a counselor or therapist can ease the hardest parts of a split. The blow to your self-esteem or the aftermath of cheating can be hard to get through. And if you have unhealthy coping mechanisms, like drinking, those tend to creep up after this sort of thing.

Exercise.

If it works for you, breaking a sweat will give your brain a boost it sorely needs. And there's nothing better than feeling and looking good for your next adventures. Or just reliving the montage from Rocky III.

Take a vacation.

Exploring a new place will refresh your mind and give you new, happy solo memories as a singleton. And maybe talking up a cutie for a temporary fling will boost your ego.

Date . . . again!

When you're ready to date again, start slowly. Dust off the old online profile or just go out with a few single friends. If you meet someone and they come on too strong, be honest about your recent breakup (if you want to be) and that you're not interested.

Embrace the past.

People think they need to be with someone forever to be in a "successful" relationship, but loving and being loved for a few years can really change people for the better. Define your own success and realize the good that might have come out of the experience.

Splitting up is a part of life, so you're not alone. Something like 90% of all art, music, or literature ever made is about the terrible parts of love (we didn't check the numbers, because whatever, it would take a long time to count). See it as an opportunity to be a better partner in the future and to get closer to what you want in life. 'Tis better to have loved and gotten consensually laid than to never have had it at all.

**The Future Awaits //
Staying Together**

You wake up every morning smelling your partner's bad breath and B.O. and you think, "This is wonderful." That's the dream, kids. It's not like the movies. We mean, it can be like the movies, but the editors always cut out all the farting and deciding whose turn it is to clean the litter box. Then you can go out on that magical sexy vacation to Italy. But first, here are the things that keep the love strong for years and years:

Focusing on the good.

Don't dwell on mistakes if the good outweighs the bad. Yes, your partner forgot your birthday once, but they were really stressed out! That project at work was killing their will to live and they made up for it later with cookies (we're easy to please, even hypothetically).

Don't forget each other.

Do nice things for each other, even if it's just remembering to buy their bunion removal cream. Knowing someone has your back (and your bunions) makes you closer.

Show affection.

That kiss when you come home from work can make all the difference in your day. It doesn't erase the fact that Paul from HR is a huge %$^ face, but it helps.

Be a cheerleader.

Showing sincere happiness when something good happens to your partner strengthens your bond. It's necessary to support them in the bad times, but you need to be there for the good ones, too (even if you don't have good news to share).

Keep talking.

You may think there's nothing to say on a given day, and that may be true sometimes. But make an effort to communicate and find new things to talk about.

Enjoy things together.

Time to yourselves is always good, but the whole point of this thing is to have a partner in crime. Make it a point to find both old and new things to do together. You gotta keep makin' memories.

Speaking of memories.

Long-term relationships allow couples to develop "interconnected memory systems." That's fancy science talk for your memories being more vivid when you recall them together because your partner will help you fill the gaps. Even for things that only happened to you. It's a superpower, basically.

Keepin' it hot.

Couples in long-term relationships often complain that their sex life is a dud or the drive is low, but sometimes it's a matter of figuring out what's changed. Maybe you need a visit to your friendly, local sex shop. We're not you, we don't know what's going on down there. Talk about what you want with your partner. Don't let shame and resentment get in the way.

Timing the sexytimes.

Sure, everyone thinks they're supposed to have the best sex on Valentine's Day after a huge steak dinner and drinks, but does that even make sense? Remember what Shakespeare said about sex and alcohol. If not, Google those three things. What? Nothing weird could possibly come up.

Not just about you.

Both of you will have long-term aspirations and an idea of your ideal self. Be there for each other to make those things happen.

Long-term relationships are hard to maintain, but it is possible. Like with heart disease or diabetes, sometimes taking small steps every day can keep both of you healthy (and keep the divorce lawyer away). Don't let everyday gripes get in the way of what really matters—you need someone to plot evil world domination with you. It's really hard to do alone.

Happy Couples

 **5:1**

HAPPY COUPLE RATIO

HAPPY COUPLES HAVE 5 POSITIVE INTERACTIONS *for* **EVERY NEGATIVE ONE.**

 **0.8:1**

DIVORCED COUPLE RATIO

COUPLES WHO ULTIMATELY
DIVORCED
HAVE JUST 0.8 HAPPY ENCOUNTERS
FOR EVERY ONE NEGATIVE INTERACTION.

THE DETERMINING FACTOR IN WHETHER COUPLES FEEL SATISFIED
WITH **THE SEX, ROMANCE, & PASSION**
IN THIER MARRIAGE IS, BY **70%**

THE QUALITY OF THEIR FRIENDSHIP WITH EACH OTHER

HAPPY COUPLES TALK MORE
PEOPLE IN THE MOST SUCCESSFUL MARRIAGES
SPEND 5 MORE HOURS
A WEEK BEING TOGETHER *and* TALKING

Cultivate positive interactions every day

GIVE A COMPLIMENT

SHOW YOUR APPRECIATION FOR SOMETHING BIG (OR SMALL)

RELIVE A FUN MEMORY

DO SOMETHING NICE FOR THEM

Source: Happify

SAVE
the
DATE

**The Future Awaits //
Long-Term Love**

If the work that goes into a long-term relationship doesn't scare you, then you're on your way to a life of happiness.

Marriage

End of the line, pal. Do it or don't.

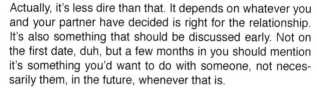

Actually, it's less dire than that. It depends on whatever you and your partner have decided is right for the relationship. It's also something that should be discussed early. Not on the first date, duh, but a few months in you should mention it's something you'd want to do with someone, not necessarily them, in the future, whenever that is.

But do you want to get married at all? Marriage ties you to another human being legally, financially, and socially. It's up to you to decide whether that's until death, but the assumption is that it should be. You're taking on a whole set of responsibilities that come with loving another human being and suddenly nearly all your decisions involve another person. It's a lot to handle. Not to mention their family is suddenly your family, and that means you're obligated to care about them, too. You need to be willing to adapt to each other's changes over time and the changes that the world throws at you.

When a marriage doesn't work, you undergo the painful (and sometimes costly) process of getting divorced. If it does, you get a best friend and someone to share the ups-and-downs of life with you.

If you go for it, make sure your partner is someone who's 100% in for the ride. And the only way to know is to evaluate your experiences dating them.

Partnership

Staying together without getting married is becoming more and more popular, so don't exclude it as an option. You can live a long and happy life together, even have kids, without ever throwing a wedding party. Some people don't like the values that marriage represents, and that's absolutely fine.

There are a few downsides, but they're manageable. You'll miss out on many legal benefits that only married couples get, so factor that into your decision.

And it's still not the most common practice. Your friends and family may give not-so-subtle hints that marriage should be on your radar. They'll give up in time. Actually, we don't know, but good luck!

Monogamy

Being in love or having sex with one person for the rest of your life is taken as a given in marriage, but some studies into human sexuality show that it may be a drawback. If you want to get married or commit to someone, but don't agree with those values, go ahead and make your own rules. It may make your marriage more stable and happy in the long run—everyone is different.

There are a few good practices to keep in mind, though. Make sure you and your partner are completely okay with and aware of each other's behavior. Pick good, healthy partners outside of the relationship and use protection to avoid diseases. Tell all your partners about your non-monogamous commitment. Not everyone is up for that. Get tested regularly for STDs and STIs. Communicate with your spouse or partner partner to make sure they don't feel neglected. Lastly, keep up with your original commitment. Your primary partner or spouse should always come first.

Kids?

It's hard to measure whether having children will make you happier. They're time-consuming, require a ton of money, and you can't break up with them. But raising them can also bring love, joy, and pride. It's safe to say that whatever problems are in your marriage before kids come along will only increase once they arrive. Studies show that kids, especially in their childhood years, are a huge stressor on marriages. Other studies show that overall, childless couples are just as happy as couples with kids. It's really a full-time job, and it's your choice whether to do it. Like Louis C.K. said: he'd die for his kids, but it's really boring to play Monopoly with them sometimes.

If you want kids, but marriage sounds undesirable, consider a partnership. A lot of couples prefer to co-parent without needing to tie the knot. And some co-parents take the romantic commitment out of the picture as well.

When it comes to your dating life, don't take this question lightly. Make sure you and your partner are on the same page. No, your dog is not a trial run. And don't be upset if they have different opinions on kids—it's a mixed bag, even for the happiest parents.

Date forever!

There's no rule saying you have to commit to one person, though that seems to be society's golden rule. Ignore it if it doesn't make you happy. Eternal bachelor and bachelorette-hood is a perfectly reasonable decision, but there are a few things to keep in mind.

Most people won't respect your decision, especially if you're a woman. A man is always a bachelor, while a woman becomes a "spinster" after an arbitrary age. You may be considered unstable or flaky because you don't want to find "the one."

The other side of the coin is that most people hold these expectations for themselves as strongly as they want to impose them on you. It's on you to be as clear as possible that you aren't interested in marriage or a partnership. You don't want to be the cause of a string of broken hearts. Still, some people may not get the message and will date you anyway. It'll be a headache, for sure.

You get to decide how long you want to be single. There's no shame in it and no one should pressure you into being part of the majority. Date, date, date until you drop. We'll be here to guide you every time.

A NOTE FROM THE AUTHORS

Dating is a weird and sometimes overwhelming rite of passage for adults, but it's also a lot of fun. These hacks are intended to keep you open to new adventures, but also safe. Trust your gut when it comes to a partner. While we've done our best to be as thorough as possible in describing all the ups-and-downs you may encounter, the truth is that life is unpredictable. We hope you give our hacks a shot, tweet the ones you love (#DatingHacks) and write to us @mangomediainc about your weird, sweet, or downright scary dating stories. Good luck finding love or whatever else you're looking for!

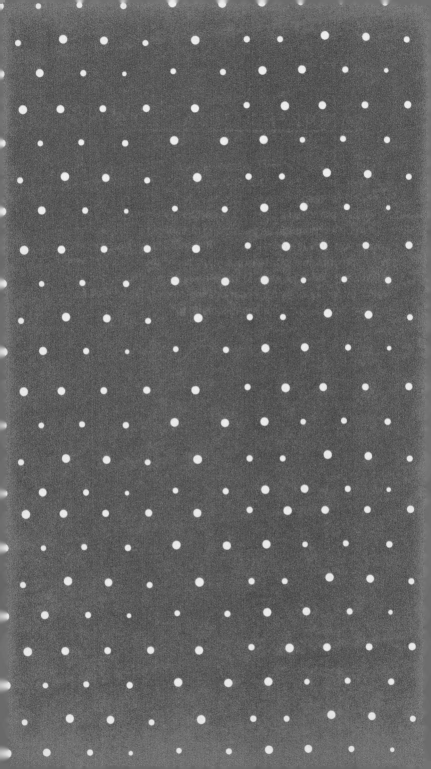

DATA SOURCES

http://www.wired.com/2014/02/how-to-create-good-online-dating-profile/#slide-id-410231:full

http://clover.co/blog/top-first-date-hot-spots

http://www.stateofdatingreport.com/findings.html

http://www1.pcmag.com/media/images/373960-infographic-break-up-with-your-partner-not-your-private-data.jpg?thumb=y

http://www.cdc.gov/violenceprevention/nisvs/infographic.html

http://visual.ly/your-body-love?utm_source=visually_embed

http://www.cdc.gov/violenceprevention/nisvs/infographic.html

http://static1.1.sqspcdn.com/static/f/803157/22205841/1364133843390/7_ways_to_improve_your_relationship.jpg?token=axo3ou55%2BuQL%2F95Z2RxcYT4qRdo%3D

http://www.scienceofrelationships.com/storage/The_Politics_of_Love.jpg?__SQUARESPACE_CACHEVERSION=1352851791367

OTHER SOURCES

http://www.plannedparenthood.org/

http://adoption.com/

http://www.fns.usda.gov/wic/women-infants-and-children-wic

http://www.rainn.org

http://www.lovingfromadistance.com/thingsforldrcouplestodo.html

http://www.ldrmagazine.com/blog/2014/06/15/130-things-to-do-together-online-real-time/

http://lifehacker.com/top-10-essential-tips-for-dating-1696547423

http://lifehacker.com/five-best-online-dating-sites-1594072317

https://kovla.com/blog/best-ideas-for-a-cheap-date/

http://www.yourtango.com/2014215261/love-dating-infographic-moving-together-5-things-you-need-know-cohabitation

https://meetville.com/blog/wp-content/uploads/2014/10/Sleeping-Guide-to-Happy-Relationship-Infographic-dating-singles-meetville-matchmaking.jpg

http://www.scienceofrelationships.com/home/2014/9/15/infographic-the-10-most-interesting-dating-studies-of-2014.html

http://www.mensfitness.com/women/dating-advice/how-do-i-strike-the-right-work-girlfriend-balance

http://www.theguardian.com/lifeandstyle/2014/sep/28/seven-secrets-of-dating-from-the-experts-at-okcupid

http://lifehacker.com/5868965/the-stupid-things-you-do-when-dating-and-how-to-fix-them

http://www.mensfitness.com/women/dating-advice/its-2014-who-should-pay-date?page=2

http://www.askmen.com/top_10/dating/signs-it-s-time-to-break-up.html

http://health.howstuffworks.com/relationships/advice/how-to-introduce-girlfriend-to-friends3.htm

http://www.loveisrespect.org/

http://www.oprah.com/relationships/New-Dating-Advice-Relationship-Expert-Tips_1

http://tech.co/background-checks-increasingly-common-online-dating-2014-01

http://health.howstuffworks.com/relationships/advice/how-to-introduce-boyfriend-to-parents3.htm

http://www.cosmopolitan.com/sex-love/advice/a31311/ask-logan-dont-like-boyfriends-friends/

http://www.glamour.com/sex-love-life/blogs/smitten/2010/12/ask-a-guy-why-wont-my-boyfrien

http://www.scienceofrelationships.com/home/2015/4/15/face-it-recover-the-self-to-recover-from-break-up.html

http://www.salon.com/2012/10/12/can_relationships_survive_different_political_views/

https://www.psychologytoday.com/blog/fulfillment-any-age/201206/the-12-ties-bind-long-term-relationships

http://time.com/3667105/make-relationship-last/

CPSIA information can be obtained at www.ICGtesting.com
Printed in the USA
BVOW11s1209110715

408095BV00005B/5/P